OH... OKAY, God!

A 30 DAY DEVOTIONAL FOR WOMEN WHO WANT TO HEAR GOD'S VOICE

BY SPARKLE JONES

Printed in the United States of America
ISBN 978-1-7337907-8-9
Sunshine Reigns Publishing Company
(A subsidiary of The Master Communicator's Writing Services)
Houston, Texas
www.mcwritingservices.com

Book Interior and Cover by Myrna Galan of Galan Graphix

Table Of Contents

Foreword

I am so proud of Sparkle Jones. She is a voice for this generation. She is one who has overcome and still overcoming anxiety, and the pressures of this world. From that journey, this book was birthed. It is very clear that Sparkle is anointed and appointed to be able to be a voice to this generation in a way that no other person could do. Her story makes her unique to the culture, and it allows her to be in tune with the times. This daily devotional is eye-opening, and is a solid piece of work. I am so proud of her, and I believe that you will be tremendously blessed by the nuggets that God has given her over these last few years. This is just the first of what is to come. There are so many more books that are going to be pulled out of Sparkle Jones and you are about to get a taste of what God is doing in her life. Are you ready? Okay, God! Let's Go!

Carlos Jones II, Pastor and Husband

Dedication

This One is For You!

Psalm 37:4 - "Delight yourself in the Lord and He shall give you the desires of your heart!"

First and foremost, I dedicate this book to God, the One who gave me the desire and ability to accomplish it. It is with the earnestness of my heart that I extend my thanks and gratitude to every person who has poured into my life, which has led me on this journey of sharing my insights with those who might find comfort and encouragement in what I have written.

Identifying each person by name would only muddy the water, and I want to be clear that each of you has played a part in what you are reading here today. I dedicate this book to you! I am grateful and appreciative. I love each of your dearly. Thank you!

Special thanks to my muse, Carlos II, Summer, Carlos III, and Carson. You were the beginning of it all!

Introduction

There was a day several years ago when I felt like all the people closest to me were going through tough seasons of their lives. I spent a lot of time sending encouraging messages and supporting them through it. At one point, it felt the load I was carrying was too much for me, and I prayed and sought God to help me navigate through it. That was when I felt God starting to speak to me through even the small occurrences in everyday situations. God would help me see connections between the things I was experiencing daily and what He wanted me to understand through those experiences. Being a mother of three gave me multiple opportunities to have these intimate conversations with God.

Over time, I would take notes about what was being revealed to me and share them because it was just too good to keep to myself. God allowed me to see so much about His goodness, grace, provision, and promises through my kids.

When I realized how God was moving through me, I understood it was time to act. The messages in this devotional have been such a blessing from God and have encouraged me and others through some challenging days. I pray that you, too, are blessed by what God has spoken through me.

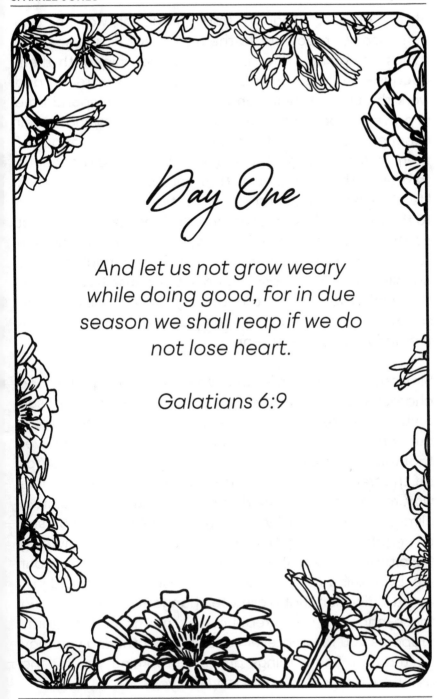

Day One

And let us not grow weary while doing good, for in due season we shall reap if we do not lose heart.

Galatians 6:9

At my church, I lead a small group of women, and periodically, I reach out to them to check in and see how things are going. I love building relationships with them because it allows me to see how they navigate life and work through the highs and the lows. I often spend time in prayer for each of them because when they share their experiences, I can see the cycles and seasons that each of them is in. One of my prayers is that God would continue to keep His hand on them in that particular season of their life. One morning, during my prayer time for them, I began to think about life's seasons, and God showed me that just as the earth goes through seasons, we, too, go through seasons, and whatever it is we are "weathering" impacts our climate. Climate is so important because that's one of the pieces that is a constant where you live. If you are in the south, you can expect warm temperatures and moisture in the air for most of the year.

Similarly, our life's climate, speaks to the quality and character of who we are. Our personal climate is based on the patterns we follow and how our experiences reflect our norms and values. There are some seasons in our lives that will feel like a personal winter, but just as the leaves fall off the trees, you have to allow yourself to shed the same way, removing the things that are impacting your spiritual climate and keeping you from blossoming. Rid yourself of negative thinking, bad attitudes, burdens, or anything toxic that will prevent new seasons from flourishing in your life. Everything is not a cause for frustration. It could just be an indication that a climate change is needed. Making those changes and creating new norms and patterns prepares you for whatever season or weathering you may go through. Some things are just grooming you for the beautiful things God has in store for you.

Reflection:

What areas of your climate could benefit from a change in your spiritual climate?

_____

_____

_____

_____

_____

_____

_____

_____

_____

_____

_____

_____

Day Two

Weeping may endure for a night, but joy comes in the morning.

Psalm 30:5 (NKJV)

A few years ago, my daughter had to have her tonsils removed. I can remember the days leading up to surgery. She was constantly sick and in a lot of pain. Her school nurse called me several times a week to say that she had come in to be checked because of her discomfort. I called her doctor, and after examining her, she explained that her tonsils needed to be taken out soon or the pain and discomfort would worsen. On the day of surgery, she had some excitement because she knew that once this was over, she wouldn't be in pain anymore. They called us to go back and see her after the surgery. Once she got into the recovery room, she began to cry out in pain. This wasn't a typical cry; this cry was one of misery. I felt terrible because I felt like I was responsible for her pain. As a mom, it's tough to see your little one in pain and unable to do anything to help. But then I realized that her pain was only temporary. What she was experiencing beforehand would have been more painful in the long run and would have repeated itself over and over again. She would have been in a constant, ongoing cycle of pain.

There are times when we make a decision, and it causes us to question if we made the right choice because sometimes, the temporary pain hurts so bad that it seems like the wrong decision. But, if we push through it, there's healing on the other side. No more suffering! Once my daughter got through the first few days of recovery, her pain was gone, and her health was restored. The thing that caused her so much pain was gone, and though it hurt for a little while, she felt much better in the end. God can remove that which causes you so much turmoil. Make the choice today to work towards your healing. Push through your temporary pain while God restores you. Let His word be your pain medicine. Now, rejoice! The sun will come out "tomorrow."

Reflection:

Are there temporary pains you are dealing with that need to be removed for you to have total healing?

_____

_____

_____

_____

_____

_____

_____

_____

_____

_____

_____

_____

_____

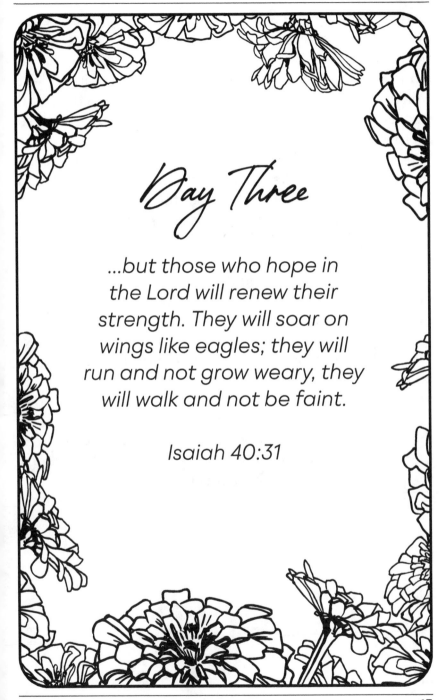

Day Three

...but those who hope in the Lord will renew their strength. They will soar on wings like eagles; they will run and not grow weary, they will walk and not be faint.

Isaiah 40:31

One morning, on my way to work, I got caught behind an accident scene. Anyone who has ever had to fight through traffic understands what this means. What is usually a 4 to 5 min drive turned into 44 very long minutes of impatient waiting. I was frustrated, but all I could think was that God was protecting me from something. You know, in those moments, you have to stay focused on the good so that your thoughts don't get stuck on the bad. Little did I know that I would need to keep that same line of thinking later in the day when I had to head to a doctor's appointment and got caught in yet another accident. I had decided that I was not waiting the second time around. I didn't want to wait, and I wasn't going to wait. I started thinking of a way to go around. Then, God gently tapped me on the shoulder and said, "Wait." Within seconds, the emergency crew moved, and traffic opened up.

What occurred to me was that there are situations we will go through that we won't want to wait patiently. We will get tired and frustrated with being in that position, but God is saying if we just wait, He'll move those roadblocks out of the way. Going around doesn't get us through it, and often, it takes us off the path where God protects us. It prolongs the process. We just have to trust God and wait!

Reflection:

What roadblocks in your life are you trying to avoid?

_____

_____

_____

_____

_____

_____

_____

_____

_____

_____

_____

_____

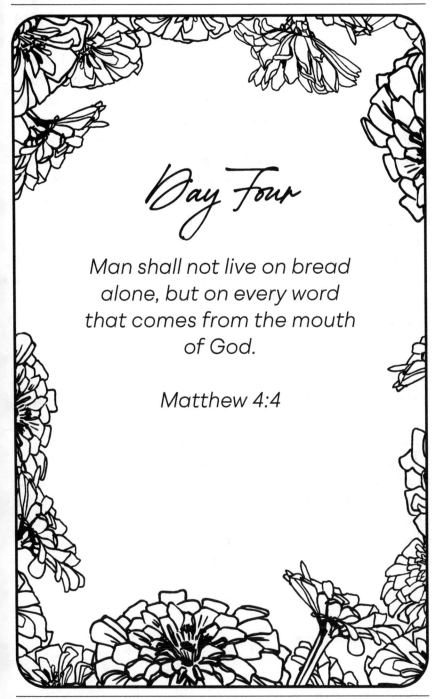

Day Four

Man shall not live on bread alone, but on every word that comes from the mouth of God.

Matthew 4:4

It had been one of those mornings, but only by prayer and moving quickly, I was leaving the house with just enough time to make it to work right at my expected arrival time. I strapped my youngest son in his car seat, loaded my things, and backed out of the driveway only to get the notification that I had "--- miles to empty." While I silently screamed inside, it suddenly it dawned on me that this is how we often operate in the spiritual. We wait until we are low on spiritual fuel, almost burned out, to try to refuel. We get those warning signals on life's road; our reactions to certain situations tell us that we need to regroup, our attitude reminds us that we need to tap into our spiritual power source. How easily we become discouraged indicates that we need some encouragement, but much like I did with my fuel warning, we ignore it convincing ourselves that we could make it a little farther. The danger in that is that we can't always make it. The fumes we operate on burn out, and so do we.

It is of the utmost importance to your spiritual health that you refuel yourselves with the word of God. Consistently, you have to turn on your Jesus music (as the kids say!), get a book, and read God's word so you can be refueled and ready to keep pushing. Make a pit stop in a small group within your local church community or a group of friends, or simply be available for God at the start or end of your day every night. Regular maintenance prevents damage. Get filled up and see how much better you perform!

Reflection:

What differences could you see in your daily performance with a little spiritual maintenance?

_____

_____

_____

_____

_____

_____

_____

_____

_____

_____

_____

_____

Day Five

My sheep hear my voice, and I know them, and they follow me.

John 10:27

I work at an elementary school. There were often a lot of decisions that I could make on my own. Other times, the approval of an administrator was required. One day, in particular, state testing was approaching, and as the coordinator, I needed to be sure what I was about to put in place was approved. I remember leaving my office, looking to find someone to get the green light to complete my task. As I was walking down the hall, looking for an administrator, I thought I heard my Assistant Principal, so I immediately stopped in the middle of the hallway to verify. A co-worker, who was in passing, asked why I stopped so abruptly. I explained that I thought I heard his voice and wanted to be still so I could hear it clearly. As strange as it seemed, she stood still with me and waited. At that moment, it was like God said, "Do you hear me clearly?"

Isn't it so much like us to get anxious about decisions we want or need to make that we don't take the time to just be still and hear God's voice? We often create a sense of urgency for ourselves and don't leave space for God to direct us. He will guide every footstep. We just have to be still and not move in haste. God will speak and lead us, allowing us to lead others as He leads us. My co-worker followed my lead that day because she had faith in my ability to do so. Imagine the ways we could lead others if we allow God to speak, we listen, and others come along for the ride. Relinquish control and listen for His voice.

Reflection:

**What are some actions you could take that
would lead others to Christ?**

_____

_____

_____

_____

_____

_____

_____

_____

_____

_____

_____

_____

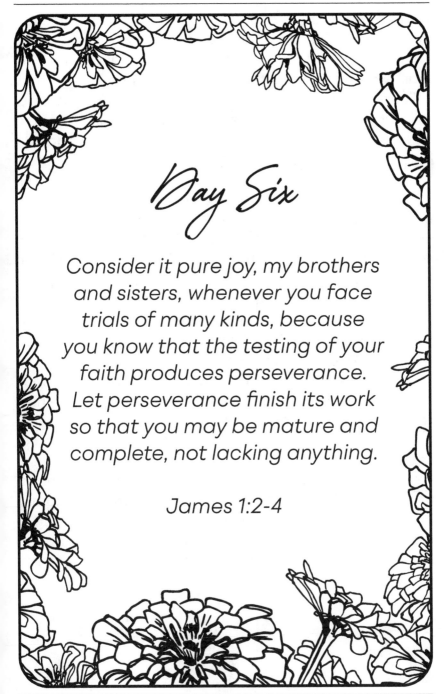

Day Six

Consider it pure joy, my brothers and sisters, whenever you face trials of many kinds, because you know that the testing of your faith produces perseverance. Let perseverance finish its work so that you may be mature and complete, not lacking anything.

James 1:2-4

We went on a family outing one day, and as most places designed for kids, they had a gift shop you could stop by on the way out. My oldest son saw a stuffed animal that he really wanted to have. It was likely because it came with a lollipop. (Haha!) After a couple of days, he actually started to like it. He wanted to take it everywhere with him. One day, he went to visit his grandparents. He took the stuffed animal out of the car into the house. He decided that he wanted to give it a haircut and bath and put it in the dryer after the bath since it was still wet. After a while, his grandmother asked if it was dry yet and told him he should check on it. She expressed that the little stuffed animal had been through so much in such a short time, and he needed to ensure it was okay. My son took it out of the dryer and said it was fine. His grandmother said, "After all that, he's still smiling." Then my son said something that gave me chills. He said, "That's because nothing can take his smile away." His grandmother went on to tell him that he could learn something from that. His statement resonated with me. That little stuffed animal operated with the joy of the Lord. "Joy is not the absence of suffering, but the presence of God." Even in his suffering after being cut (hair cut) and burned (dryer), he still smiled because he had the presence of God amid suffering. When you face trials, consider it pure joy... the scripture shows us the operative word "when." That means trials will come, but joy isn't contingent on our circumstances. It's not an indicator that suffering won't happen. But it is indicative of God's presence in our lives. So, we can count it all joy when we have the presence of God!

Reflection:

How could you change the way you view the trials in your life and consider them pure joy?

_____

_____

_____

_____

_____

_____

_____

_____

_____

_____

_____

_____

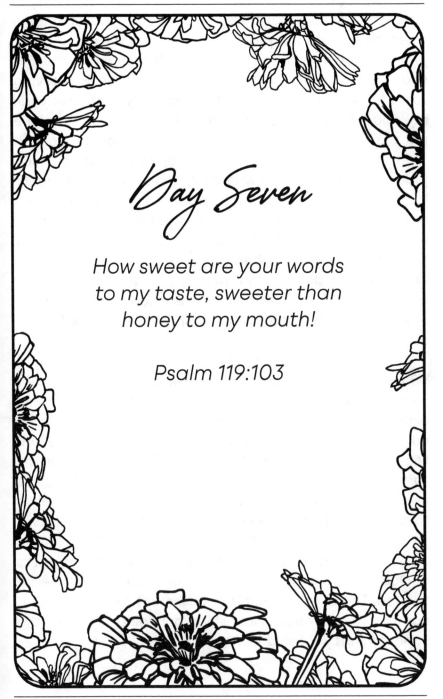

Day Seven

How sweet are your words to my taste, sweeter than honey to my mouth!

Psalm 119:103

Parents of school-aged kids understand what it means when it's science fair project time. It means that you help pick the topic, you help complete the experiment, and you help put the project board together. It's like reliving some experiences that you have already had. This year, my daughter wanted to do something with plants, so we put our thinking cap on and went to work coming up with ideas. She decided to base her project on testing which plant would grow faster when watered with various liquids. We measured and used the same amount of liquid in each plant every time we watered. As time progressed, we began to notice some changes in some of the plants. The plant nourished with vinegar became dry, and the soil began to crack and break. The plant nourished with salt water had no growth. But one of the variants was sugar water, and we observed that the plant with sugar water grew the fastest and the most.

While my daughter was learning a life science lesson, I was learning a spiritual science lesson. I am sure I have had some experience with this in the past, yet there was something new to be learned here. Salt, vinegar, and sugar represent the things we nourish our spirits with. The vinegar is all the tart and bitter things we pour into our minds that deplete us of what we need to sustain (toxic relationships, negative thinking, wasted time on meaningless things, and the list goes on!). The salt reflects our complacency; we remain in a place of no growth. But the sugar is all the sweet words of God that spark our spiritual energy and ignite our desire to grow. The Word of God is nourishment for the soul and comfort for the heart. Nourishing our spirits is one of the richest things we can do.

Reflection:

What are you watering your spirit with?

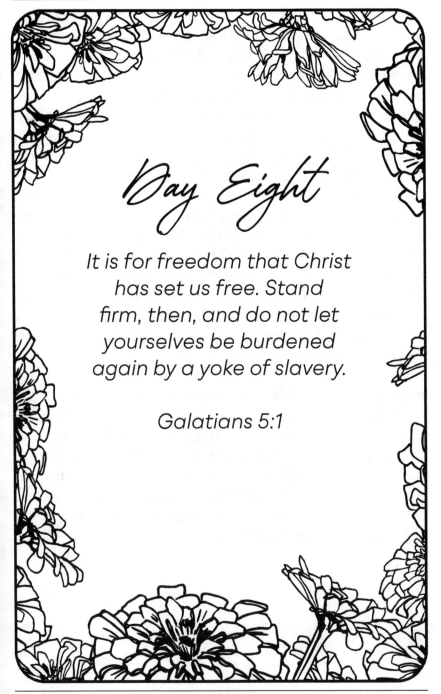

Day Eight

It is for freedom that Christ has set us free. Stand firm, then, and do not let yourselves be burdened again by a yoke of slavery.

Galatians 5:1

If you are or have been the parent of young kids, then you understand how impossible it seems to keep your car clean. Several days ago, I looked at my car's backseat and was completely shocked at how I had allowed clutter to build up back there. So, I decided to clean it out. I picked up one thing after another. Before I knew it, I was carrying a lot of weight, most of it from stuff that didn't even belong to me. I looked at everything I had in my arms and on my back and realized most of it belonged to my three kids. I went on to take all the stuff into the house, convinced I was strong enough to do it in one trip. I couldn't even see the floor in front of me at certain points. I was blindly carrying the weight of a bunch of stuff that wasn't even mine. I even stumbled a couple of times because everything started tripping me up. Then God said, "Why do you feel you need to carry all that? Release it." So, I did. I dropped it right where I stood. I had the kids come get what was theirs, and I only carried my own stuff.

If we are honest, this is the same position we are often in spiritually, carrying everyone else's weight. We hold it until we are broken or crumbling. But sometimes, you have to just release the weight. Release means to escape confinement. Break free from being confined to the problems of others. You don't have to carry it on your own. Bolster your boundaries to protect your well-being. You can't pour from an empty cup.

Reflection:

What weights are you blindly carrying that you need to release?

_____

_____

_____

_____

_____

_____

_____

_____

_____

_____

_____

_____

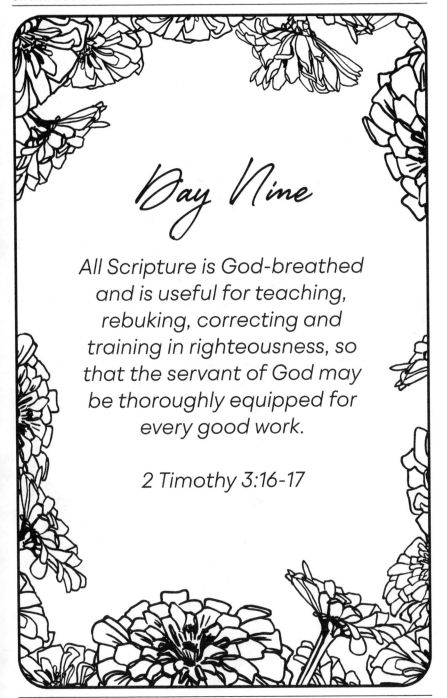

Day Nine

*All Scripture is God-breathed
and is useful for teaching,
rebuking, correcting and
training in righteousness, so
that the servant of God may
be thoroughly equipped for
every good work.*

2 Timothy 3:16-17

On Thursday evenings, I lead a small group of women. More often than not, when we meet, our end time is after my kids' bedtime. This can sometimes be challenging because they look forward to me praying with them and giving hugs and kisses before bed. Since the start of the pandemic, my group would meet virtually, allowing me to be home pretty close to bedtime. Of course, there were some nights when the topics were deep, the conversation was good, and the night went a little long. One night, not long ago, this was the case. Surprisingly, I heard a knock on the office door, and when I opened it, my oldest two kids stood there. They came into the room to share something with me before bed. They said they were too excited to sleep, so they had to share. They went on to tell me that they both read Bible stories for their reading time that evening. My son said, "Mommy, the Bible makes you feel good. It changes you." My daughter went on to say that they didn't fight the whole night. They helped each other, shared their things with one another, and said kind words to each other. The excitement in their voice made my heart happy.

If at ages 7 and 5, this is what the word of God will do for you, imagine the joy and comfort His word brings for adults that understand the depths of what they read. If the Word improved their relationship after an hour of reading, what could it do for your friendships, working relationships, or marriages if you tapped in every day? God's word is an operations manual that provides the ultimate guidance for life. Everything you need is at your fingertips!

Reflection:

How can you use God's word to change the relationships in your life positively?

Day Ten

He heals the brokenhearted and binds up their wounds.

Psalm 147:3

One night, I was taking my youngest son to bed when I heard what sounded like fuzz and static. I stopped on the catwalk to see where it was coming from, but I thought, "It's probably the TV." I dismissed it, took him to his room and laid him down, and went on to finish preparing for the next day. Around midnight, my son woke up crying (which is unusual, especially around that time), so I went up to check on him and get him back to sleep. When I left the room, I heard the sound again. I searched the house inside and outside, trying to figure it out. Standing on the catwalk, concerned and confused, I looked up. I saw what looked like water, but I wasn't sure exactly what it was because it looked like it could have been a shadow. When I turned on the light, I saw that it was water! Water had been running from the attic into the ceiling and walls. God had allowed me to hear the warning sign, and I dismissed it. When he didn't have my attention, he sent a new sign through my son's cries that brought me back to the first signal. If I had just listened the first time, I could have spared us some of the damage.

Sometimes there's a deeper personalized message in the situations we encounter, and we have to ask ourselves, "What could God be speaking to me through what occurred?" It is so important that we don't miss the signs that God is sending us. He may simply be showing you that he can repair what's broken before it's destroyed. Your dismissal of a situation, circumstance, or issue doesn't mean it's done. Damage doesn't always mean destruction. God can restore all things.

Reflection:

**Can you think of any warning
signs God is signaling to you?**

_____

_____

_____

_____

_____

_____

_____

_____

_____

_____

_____

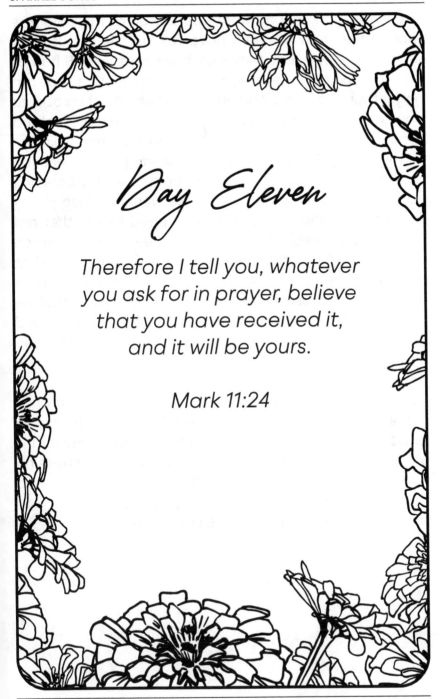

Day Eleven

Therefore I tell you, whatever you ask for in prayer, believe that you have received it, and it will be yours.

Mark 11:24

As a working mom, I do what I can to be at my children's appointments to ensure I have full details about their health and any needs they may have. Last week, I had to take my kids to the eye doctor. I had a meeting that ran longer than expected, and I just knew I would not be able to leave when I had hoped to. Once I got to the car, I realized I was running much later than planned, but I was going to try my best to be on time. I had picked up my oldest son first and was enroute to get my daughter. We kept getting stopped by so many red lights. We were so close to my daughter's school when we got stopped by another red light! Seconds later, the light turned green. I heard my son say, "Thank you, God, for hearing my prayer." I asked what he was praying about. He said he prayed for the lights to turn green because we needed to go. He shared that he prayed to himself, but not out loud at first. Then, he prayed out loud, and the light changed. He said, "All I had to do was say it out loud."

I was so touched because I watched my 6-year-old child put his faith into practice. He knew all he had to do was go to God with what he needed, and God would answer his prayers. His faith in God was boosted that day because he watched God work it out. Our faith should be no different. If He did it before, He can do it again! Stop holding your requests hostage and go to the Lord in prayer.

Reflection:

What prayers have you been keeping to yourself that you need God to work out for you?

_____

_____

_____

_____

_____

_____

_____

_____

_____

_____

_____

_____

_____

_____

_____

_____

_____

_____

_____

_____

_____

_____

_____

_____

_____

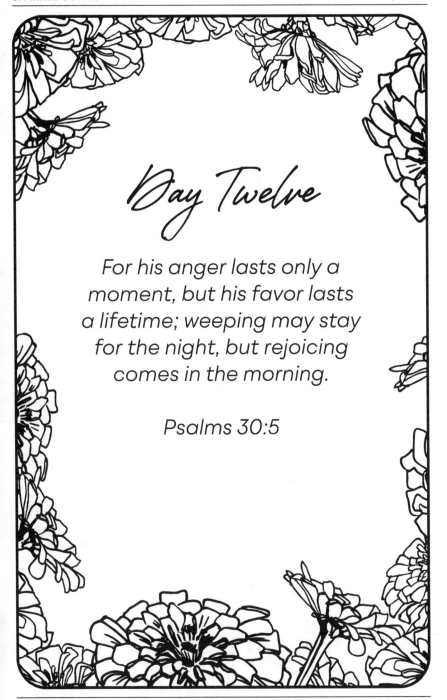

Day Twelve

For his anger lasts only a moment, but his favor lasts a lifetime; weeping may stay for the night, but rejoicing comes in the morning.

Psalms 30:5

Some days, by the end of the night, I am exhausted. Typically, I am up early before anyone else in my house, preparing breakfast and lunches, go to work all day, come home to cook dinner, help with homework, clean, do laundry, and so on! There are days when I have moments where I just don't feel like going to work the next day. On those days I am usually dealing with a 'to-do' list, or working towards how I will conquer all the anxious thoughts that come to haunt me. If I am honest, there are days when I am filled with complaints, and I have to stop myself from being so negative. I had one of those days recently. I went to bed full of complaints. I prayed and went to sleep. The next morning, my youngest son woke up, came downstairs, and with a great deal of excitement, said, "Mommy! I woke up!" He was so excited to be awake. It was the purest form of 'joy in the morning.' I smiled and got excited with him because waking up is a daily blessing.

It's so easy to get caught up in life's stressors, challenges, and anxieties that we forget to be thankful for the little things. And that is exactly what I had done. I was so focused on what was not going well that I forgot to even acknowledge God for all that was going right. My son's joy about waking up was such a beautiful reminder that there is much to be thankful for, and although obstacles may come, God's joy is ever present within us. Walk into today knowing that our God performs millions of little miracles daily, and we are not exempt from His miraculous power. I may have wept last night, but I was restored with joy this morning!!

Reflection:

Make a list of all the little things you have to be grateful for.

_____

_____

_____

_____

_____

_____

_____

_____

_____

_____

_____

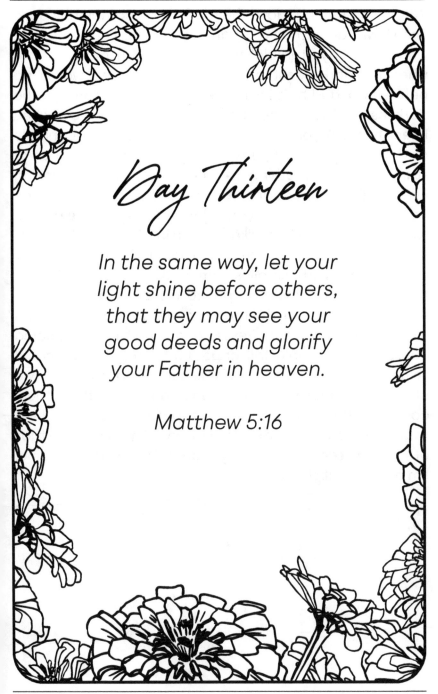

Day Thirteen

In the same way, let your light shine before others, that they may see your good deeds and glorify your Father in heaven.

Matthew 5:16

When I'm sleeping, I love the room to be completely dark. The downside is that you can't see where you are going, what you may stumble over, or what you may run into when it's dark. Most mornings, my husband wakes up before I do, and he tries his best to navigate through the darkness, but it can be challenging. There are days when I hear him kick something the kids have left in the middle of the floor or yell out in pain when he has stepped on or stumbled into something. This morning, as he tried making his way through our dark room, he decided to turn on the flashlight on his phone. Almost immediately, I woke up due to the light. As much as I like to sleep in complete darkness, there is beauty in this situation. God showed me just how powerful even the smallest amount of light could be in the midst of darkness. I opened my eyes, and even on the opposite side of the room, I could see the tricycle on the floor, the door, the dresser, and everything that could cause me to stumble, fall, or get hurt. Imagine if we could shine our light in the midst of this dark world. Imagine if we all could illuminate when there was darkness so that others could see their stumbling blocks, pitfalls, and everything that could cause them pain. Let your light shine so that others may see Christ through you. This little light of mine, I'm gonna let it shine!

Identify some ways that you could let your light shine for others to see Christ.

_____

_____

_____

_____

_____

_____

_____

_____

_____

_____

_____

_____

_____

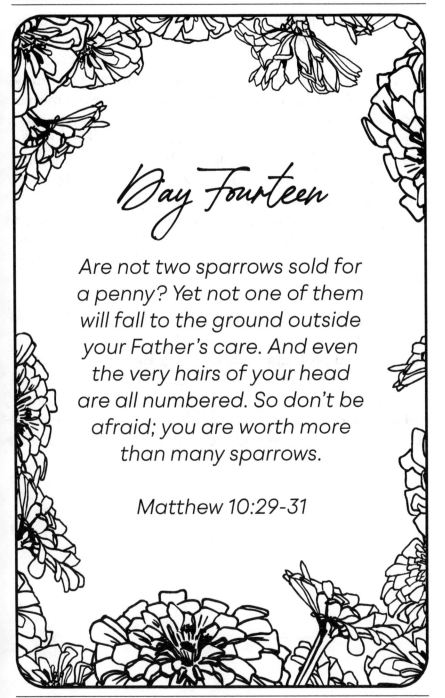

Day Fourteen

Are not two sparrows sold for a penny? Yet not one of them will fall to the ground outside your Father's care. And even the very hairs of your head are all numbered. So don't be afraid; you are worth more than many sparrows.

Matthew 10:29-31

I was loading the car to leave for work a couple of days ago when I noticed a baby bird on the street at the end of our driveway. It was evident that the baby bird could not fly. It is hard to say if the bird was hurt or just not ready for flight . What caught my attention most was the mama bird hovering over the baby bird, protecting it at all costs. The mama bird knew her baby was hurt or unable to fly. She knew that if left there alone, the baby bird wouldn't survive. A bird's natural response to oncoming traffic when resting on a road or the ground is to fly away when there is oncoming traffic . In this case, even with the sound of road noise and every passing car, the mama bird continuously surveyed her surroundings but never budged from standing guard over her baby.

I realized that God loves us just the same, if not more. When we're hurt, broken, or unprepared for what may come our way, God protects us at all costs. He is not moved or bothered by the attacks of the enemy or the darts he sends to destroy us. He is our father, and He's doing what fathers do; protecting and covering us in every situation. That's the kind of love and protection that only God can provide. We are safe in His arms.

Reflection:

Name some of the ways that God has protected you in the last week.

_____

_____

_____

_____

_____

_____

_____

_____

_____

_____

_____

_____

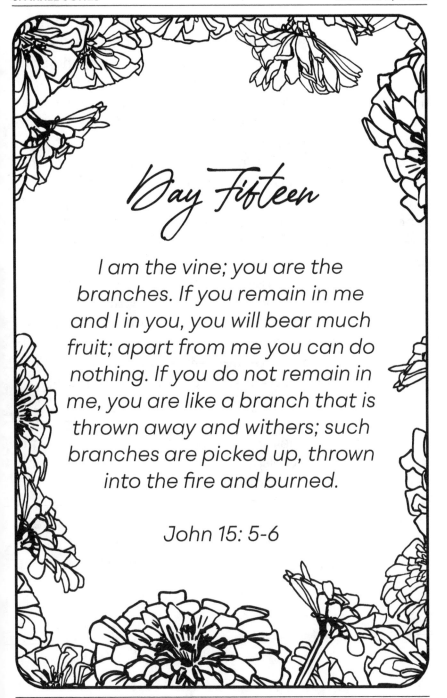

Day Fifteen

I am the vine; you are the branches. If you remain in me and I in you, you will bear much fruit; apart from me you can do nothing. If you do not remain in me, you are like a branch that is thrown away and withers; such branches are picked up, thrown into the fire and burned.

John 15: 5-6

Several years ago, I wanted to support a little girl that I love dearly. She suffers from alopecia and over time she lost the majority of her hair. This brought about teasing and hard times for her at school. It would break my heart to hear her mom share some of what she had been feeling and experiencing. I really wanted to help her navigate this time in her life. I decided I would cut my hair to donate to her. My decision was certainly a move that was bigger than me. Once it was done, I had cut off about 16 inches of hair. This certainly was a drastic change. This decision came with shock, adjustments, and acceptance. I wasn't used to the new me. Fast forward a few years later, my hair had grown, and I was much more comfortable with myself. It wasn't long before I faced another challenge. My hair became badly damaged from heat. I cried. I questioned the reason for this setback. I asked God what I needed to learn from the experience. While the answer wasn't revealed to me immediately, I took better care of my hair during this time than I ever have. I made restoring my hair a top priority.

I realized that God was showing me that growth can't happen without pruning. You have to cut the dead weight (dead ends) off, nourish what has been damaged, and watch the new and better you grow. There are tough seasons, but no season remains forever; in some, you will remove what's been damaged by life's storms; in others, you will flourish. But, as long as you're connected to the vine, the time, energy, and effort you invest into your spirit will reap healthy spiritual growth.

Reflection:

What areas of your life could benefit from being connected to the vine for you to experience growth?

_____

_____

_____

_____

_____

_____

_____

_____

_____

_____

_____

_____

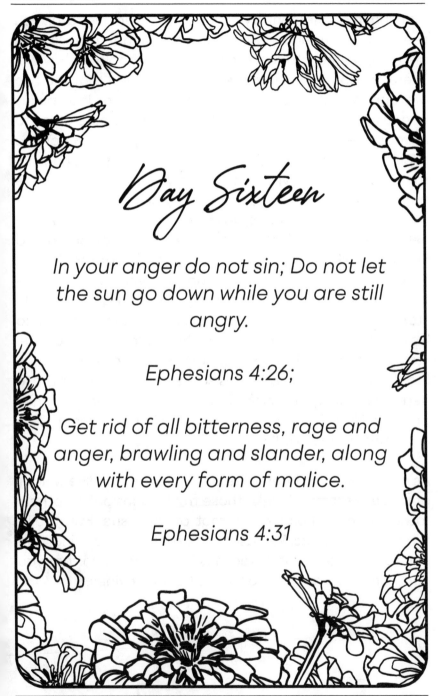

Day Sixteen

In your anger do not sin; Do not let the sun go down while you are still angry.

Ephesians 4:26;

Get rid of all bitterness, rage and anger, brawling and slander, along with every form of malice.

Ephesians 4:31

Working in an elementary school as an administrator, you see a lot of students dealing with emotional distress I You also see some students exhibit undesirable behaviors. There are some cases where you understand that the two are connected. I have always had an open-door policy because I wanted students to feel they had a safe place to retreat if needed and teachers to feel they had someone to support them in challenging moments. It was not unusual to have students visit me because of an undesirable behavior. A student once stopped by because his teacher said he had hit another student. Once we started talking, he opened up that his parents were recently divorced and his mom had lost his baby brother (miscarriage). He began to share that he comes to school stressed every day. He feels like no one likes him and others are mean to him. He started to cry. I had some blown-up balloons in my office, so we grabbed a couple, and I asked him to follow me outside. I told him that one balloon was sadness and one was anger. I told him to pop the balloons so we could get rid of those negative feelings. He stomped on each balloon until they popped. He said, "No more sadness. No more anger. Only happiness inside now!"

As adults, we also internalize and carry around the weight of those feelings. We take those frustrations out on others rather than addressing the root of the issue. Eventually, that pressure busts. Release the pressure by 'popping' and destroying the negative feelings in your heart so that you can work towards the healing that God provides.

Reflection:

What negative feelings do you need to 'pop' and destroy?

_____

_____

_____

_____

_____

_____

_____

_____

_____

_____

_____

_____

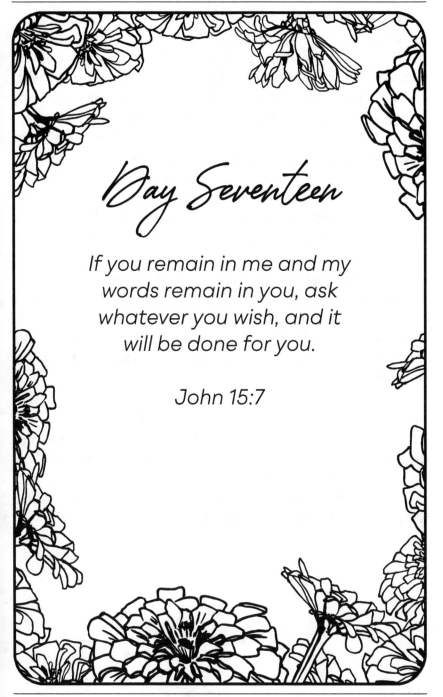

Day Seventeen

If you remain in me and my words remain in you, ask whatever you wish, and it will be done for you.

John 15:7

I have mentioned before that I have an open-door policy at work. You can greatly impact kids when you make yourself available to them. It also helps with building relationships, and spreading love and kindness. There is a student who comes by my office daily to check on me and ask how I'm doing. One day he stopped by, and I acknowledged his Spiderman jacket. It was a cool jacket! I mentioned to him that my son would love to have that jacket. He shared the name of the brand with me so I could find one for my son. I thanked him for being so caring every day and sharing about his jacket, and then he headed back to class. This kid really loved spending time with me, so he would pop in a few times a day to check on me. Well, as I mentioned, the jacket was really cool, so after he left, I looked up the jacket online, and it was out of stock. Later that day, the student returned and asked if I had ordered it for my son. I explained that it was out of stock. This young man took off his jacket to hand me and said, "Here, your son can have my jacket." It was the sweetest thing!

At that moment, God showed me that this is exactly what He does for us. He checks in. He makes sure we're good. He enjoys spending time with us. He meets our needs! All we have to do is talk to Him, acknowledge His presence, and tell him what we need. "What a friend we have in Jesus... what a privilege to carry everything to God in prayer."

Reflection:

What do you need to carry to God in prayer?

_____

_____

_____

_____

_____

_____

_____

_____

_____

_____

_____

_____

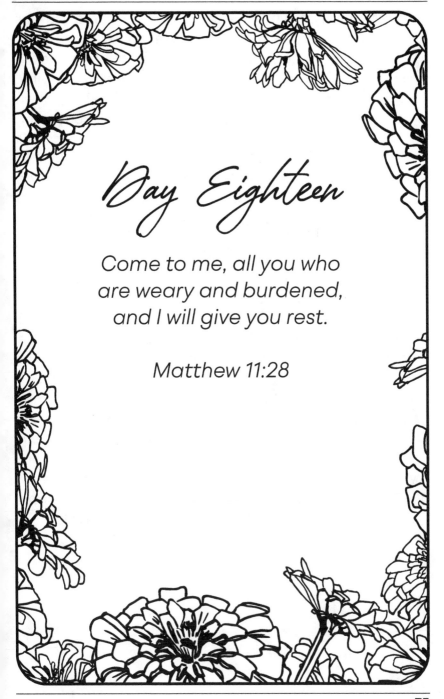

Day Eighteen

Come to me, all you who are weary and burdened, and I will give you rest.

Matthew 11:28

One afternoon, my youngest son was visibly tired. He was fussy and rubbing his eyes. I took him to lay down for a nap, and the moment I walked away, he started to cry. I walked out of the room and closed the door. Still crying, he was screaming, "Mama." After a while, he slid down the side of the bed, opened the door, and came running to me. Immediately, he stopped crying, but he was still tired. I went to lay him down again, but he didn't wait this time. He slid right down off the bed, opened the door, and came straight to me. I held him until he calmed down and eventually went to sleep.

This spoke to me on a couple of different levels. God sees us in our weary moments. He knows when we're tired and needs rest. He places us in positions to get what we need, although sometimes we run from the place of rest that He has laid out for us. It's in those moments when we can't see what God is doing, and we're screaming out for Him, that we realize God was there all along. A closed door doesn't mean our access to God is locked or off limits. Sometimes we just have to walk through the door to get to the Father. And much like my son, we find that the Father is there waiting to hold us in His everlasting arms. We don't have to sit there crying, waiting to see if God is coming back to rescue us. We always have access to God. There's safety in His arms. It's time to rest while God takes care of everything else.

Reflection:

When was the last time you rested while God took care of everything else?

_____

_____

_____

_____

_____

_____

_____

_____

_____

_____

_____

_____

Day Nineteen

*For we live by faith,
not by sight.*

2 Corinthians 5:7

When you aren't a morning person, mornings can be a struggle to get yourself and three kids ready. My youngest son is at a really playful age where everything is funny to him, and he just doesn't understand how much I need him to work with me. Recently, as we were getting ready for the day, my son took off running from me. All I could hear was his laughter becoming fainter as he ran all the way back to his room. I kept telling him to come so I could get him ready. I stood close to the top of the stairs and put my arms out for him to come. He came running! I was about five steps from the top. My baby boy literally ran with no concern for the steps. He never even looked down. He just trusted that I would catch him. That hit me so hard.

I began to think how much we function in this same manner. We run from God; from his safety, plans, and protection, but no matter what, He is there with his arms outstretched, ready to receive us. If we could just trust that He will catch us, He will do the rest. My son literally walked by faith and not by sight because if he had walked by sight and looked down at his reality, he would have fallen. But God is so good that even in those moments, he swoops in and rescues us. Whatever it is that you're running from, walk by faith! He's going to catch you and carry you.

**What is God trying to get you ready
for that you're running from?**

_____

_____

_____

_____

_____

_____

_____

_____

_____

_____

_____

_____

_____

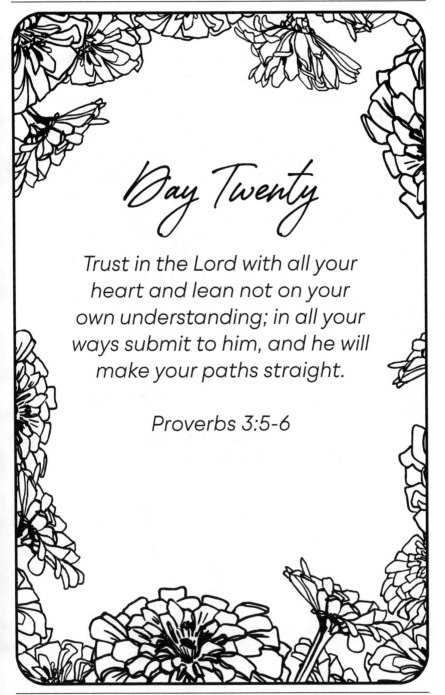

Day Twenty

Trust in the Lord with all your heart and lean not on your own understanding; in all your ways submit to him, and he will make your paths straight.

Proverbs 3:5-6

Have you ever sat back and watched how determined kids can be when they really want to do something? As a parent, I love seeing their determination, but I always want to step in and help. I'm learning to leave space for them to explore before intervening so they can learn from the process. I've seen this a number of times being a mom of three, but I had a different revelation with my youngest son. When Carson was a bit younger, he was standing on the side of the couch and decided he wanted to get on the couch. I remember watching him, seeing how determined he was to get up there on his own. He kept trying but couldn't get his leg high enough to pull himself up. I told him to come to the front of the couch so it would be easier. He kept trying from the side with no success. I sat there and watched him struggle, knowing there was an easier way, but he wasn't following my instructions. Eventually, he felt so defeated and tired he started to cry out of frustration.

It reminded me of how God lays out paths for us; somehow, we end up on our own paths. When we do things in our own way of thinking, we end up struggling and fighting unnecessarily; which often leads us to feeling defeated. God's path to get us wherever we need to be will always be easier.

Reflection:

In what ways have you gone off-path and tried to navigate life without God's help?

_____

_____

_____

_____

_____

_____

_____

_____

_____

_____

_____

Day Twenty One

For the wages of sin is death, but the gift of God is eternal life in Christ Jesus our Lord.

Romans 6:23

We were riding home one day, and my daughter saw an advertisement on the highway. The company was promoting free items. My daughter started to read the sign aloud, and part of the caption said, "Everyone loves free stuff." She immediately responded by expressing her doubts about the advertisement. She said, "They always say something is free, but it's really not. They act like they don't want to be paid, but it's basically a scam to take your money." I acknowledged that I agreed with her, and in some cases, she was correct. Most often, those promotions are a way to lure you in and entice you to buy something. You may not spend your money on that particular item they promote as 'free,' but everything else comes with a cost.

If we aren't careful and aware, that's exactly what the enemy does to us. He draws us in by tempting us with things that seem appealing, and before we know it, we've yielded to temptation, and we have to pay the price. Just because something looks good doesn't make it good for you! Be mindful of what you pay for with your time, energy, attitude, love, and attention. Satan may fool you into believing that sin comes with no cost, but nothing he has to offer is free. Get into your word so that you can combat the lies of the enemy with the truth of God's word.

Reflection:

What lies has the enemy told you to lead you into sin?

_____

_____

_____

_____

_____

_____

_____

_____

_____

_____

_____

_____

Day Twenty Two

For the LORD your God is he who goes with you to fight for you against your enemies, to give you the victory.'

Deuteronomy 20:4

Several weeks ago I had a very challenging work week. There were some pretty tough days; I even cried a few times. By Friday, I felt defeated. I kept thinking to myself and expressing to others that I was giving my all, but I still felt like I was losing. As the kids and I were riding in the truck on Friday evening, they asked how my day was. I told them that I had a really tough day. The next thing I knew, my son started singing the song 'Champion' by Maverick City Music and Upper Room. My daughter joined in with him, and they blessed and reminded me that I am undefeated. The lyrics say, "You are my champion. Giants fall when you stand undefeated. Every battle You've won. I am who You say I am. You crown me with confidence. I am seated, in the heavenly place, undefeated, with the one who has conquered it all." I thanked God right at that moment because He always uses my kids as vessels to speak a word to others through me. But, right then, He spoke a word to me. When you let the undefeated Champ fight your battles, you never lose! God is fighting for you through every battle you encounter. He is by your side when warfare is knocking at your door. He stands behind you when the enemy attacks. He has equipped you and just; when you feel defeated, He steps in and conquers it all.

Reflection:

What battles do you need God to fight for you?

_____

_____

_____

_____

_____

_____

_____

_____

_____

_____

_____

_____

Day Twenty Three

But blessed is the one who trusts in the Lord, whose confidence is in him. They will be like a tree planted by the water that sends out its roots by the stream. It does not fear when heat comes; its leaves are always green. It has no worries in a year of drought and never fails to bear fruit.

Jeremiah 17: 7-8

There are some days I am convinced that my kids think our home is the park. I'm pretty sure they see the sofas as jungle gyms, the living room as an open field, and the staircase as a slide at the park. I walked into the house one day to find my kids playing with the soccer ball in the house. I was a little confused that my husband allowed this to take place, but before I could even ask what was going on, one good kick and the ball flew across the room, knocking my Aloe Vera plant to the floor. The plant and the soil immediately came out of the pot, and it all fell apart. They hurriedly tried to scoop up the pieces and put them back into the pot. It was leaning, but it was standing. As I have mentioned before, I don't have a green thumb, so fixing it was not a skill of mine. It couldn't have been more than a day or two later the same thing happened. The kids rushed to try and pick up the pieces of the plant and the soil, but I told my daughter not to worry about putting it back into the pot because the plant was no longer rooted in the soil, and it couldn't survive like that.

This is the case for us, too. We carry on without being rooted in the Word. We become broken from every attack that comes our way, yet somehow, we still neglect to nurture or nourish our spiritual health, and the moment adversity comes, it knocks us completely off our feet. If we aren't careful, we become totally disconnected from what gives us life. You can't grow when you aren't rooted. There's no life in dead situations. It doesn't mean that you can't bring your spiritual health back to life, but you have to put in the work to restore what has been broken. We don't allow our physical health to go unattended, and we should not easily dismiss caring for our spiritual well-being. It's time to get rooted!

Reflection:

How can you nurture your spiritual life in order to gain restoration?

_____

_____

_____

_____

_____

_____

_____

_____

_____

_____

_____

_____

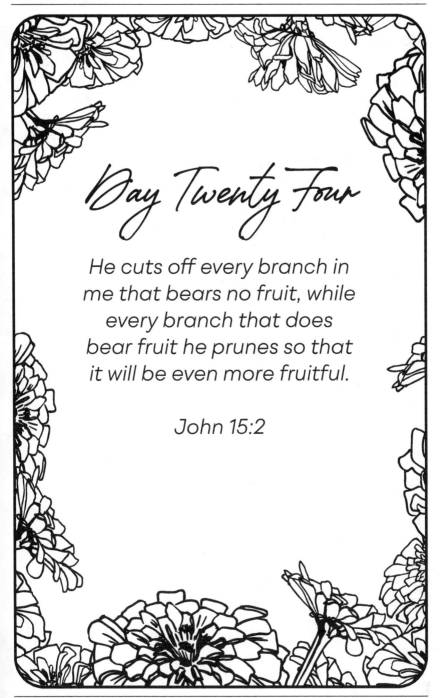

Day Twenty Four

*He cuts off every branch in
me that bears no fruit, while
every branch that does
bear fruit he prunes so that
it will be even more fruitful.*

John 15:2

Can I just start by saying that I do not have a green thumb! I have several plants, but I just was not fortunate enough to be talented in this way. I water them and give them access to light, but I can tell when my plants need some tender, loving care. I was recently watering my plants and noticed that one of them had a couple of dead leaves dangling from it. I got a little concerned that the plants would die. Without a second thought, I pruned the plant, removing everything that was no longer healthy or alive. Immediately after, the plant looked better. It didn't have the weight of all those dead leaves and stems holding it down anymore. I started to think about the pruning process and its necessity for a plant's growth. Then, I thought about the areas I would need pruning for my personal growth. I've been struggling with my hair journey for a little more than a year now, and a couple of years ago, after washing my hair, the condition caused me to be stressed. I had so much dead and damaged hair. I thought to myself, "What is this benefiting you? Let go of what's weighing you down so your hair can flourish." I realized that not only was I carrying the weight of the dead hair, but the resentment, frustration, anxiety, and stress of my hair being in this state. My hair was damaged and reminded me that situations might damage us, but growth can still occur.

So, just like I did with my plant, I took action. I pruned my hair and myself of all the dead weight, stress, and resentment I had been carrying around and revitalized myself. I felt liberated! I was released from the burdens of unhealthy hair and emotions. This gave me a new start for personal and spiritual growth.

Reflection:

What in your life needs pruning so that you can have healthy spiritual growth?

_____

_____

_____

_____

_____

_____

_____

_____

_____

_____

_____

_____

Day Twenty Five

Praise be to the God and Father of our Lord Jesus Christ, the Father of compassion and the God of all comfort.

2 Corinthians 1:3

We live in the Houston area, so it is not unusual to experience some storms in our area, especially during hurricane season. The thunder is scary for my kids every time. It usually will wake them out of their sleep because they have been startled by it. One night, it was storming, and my youngest son woke up scared. He kept screaming, "I'm so scared!" I went upstairs to comfort him and assure him everything would be fine. He had such a hard time settling down that I brought him to my room and let him lay next to me until he fell asleep again. When I got up to get dressed in the morning, he woke up and asked me not to leave him. He was still afraid to be alone in the storm. I reminded him that his dad was right next to him and would be there if he got scared again.

I walked away to get dressed with a heart of gratitude because God reminded and helped me to always be mindful that the Father never leaves us. He's with us through every storm, through every valley, and on the mountaintop. He comforts us in times of fear and holds us when we need Him the most. Sometimes, we have moments where we just need to cry out to God, and when we do, He's our present help in times of trouble. He's never out of reach. Let the Father be your comfort.

Reflection:

What storms in your life do you need God to comfort you through?

_____

_____

_____

_____

_____

_____

_____

_____

_____

_____

_____

_____

Day Twenty Six

*He heals the brokenhearted
and binds up their wounds.*

Psalm 147:3

I had surgery on my hand. A couple of weeks into my recovery, I went for a follow-up appointment. As part of the follow-up process, they had to remove the stitches. Although they took the stitches out, my hand still looked a little uneasy on the eyes as it continued to heal. Periodically, I would examine it to be sure it was healing how it should and to take notice of any changes apart from what the doctor said was normal. A few days after my appointment, I was in the car with my kids, and I asked them if they wanted to see my hand. I showed my daughter, and she instantly turned her head in disgust. My oldest son told me that it looked dirty. Then, my baby boy responded, "But it's getting better, though." He was absolutely right! I used this as a teachable moment and explained that sometimes there are certain situations where things will look worse before they look better because healing is a process.

This is true to our physical bodies, but it also applies to the heart. Some wounds are cut deep. Sometimes we get burned. And though it hurts, it does get better. The pain isn't permanent, but the healing won't always be quick. The process may cause some "ugly" moments, but if you keep nurturing the wound, you will recover. Just as you would care for and treat a wound of the flesh, you must be mindful of the things you let into your heart. No matter the source of your hurt, God can repair your wounds.

Reflection:

What wounds do you need God to heal in your life?

_____

_____

_____

_____

_____

_____

_____

_____

_____

_____

_____

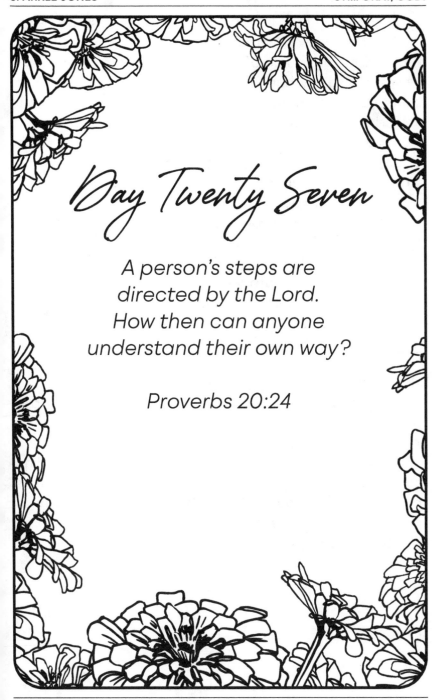

Day Twenty Seven

A person's steps are
directed by the Lord.
How then can anyone
understand their own way?

Proverbs 20:24

My kids take guitar lessons once a week. Usually, while one is in their lesson, we walk around the town center until they're done. A couple of weeks ago, my daughter was in her lesson, so my husband, my two sons, and I grabbed dinner at a restaurant in the town center. The restaurant offered free ice cream cones, so of course, the kids wanted one on the way out. As we were walking back to the music school, we had to cross the street. My husband led the way to be sure he was ahead of us in case a car came through. I was holding my youngest son in my left arm and my other arm around my oldest son as they enjoyed their ice cream. My oldest son started to slow his pace, and I encouraged him to catch up. My husband looked back and said, "Bud ain't worried about nothing but that ice cream because he knows I'll get him across safely." I got so excited!! I even thanked him for saying that because isn't that the reality we get to walk in?

We can enjoy the blessings of God and not worry about a thing because the Father always protects us, looks after us, and provides us with safety. We might need some encouragement along the way when things get tough, and we move at a different pace, but God is always leading the way and guiding us on our path. Whatever situations you're facing right now, take your focus off the problem so you can enjoy the sweet stuff because God is leading you right to where He needs you to be.

Reflection:

In what areas of your life do you need God to take the lead and guide you?

_____

_____

_____

_____

_____

_____

_____

_____

_____

_____

_____

_____

Day Twenty Eight

But he said to me, "My grace is sufficient for you, for my power is made perfect in weakness." Therefore, I will boast all the more gladly about my weaknesses, so that Christ's power may rest on me.

2 Corinthians 12:9

My vehicle has a push-button start, and I guess there is something so cool about that to my kids because they enjoy taking turns to push the button and start the truck. Not long ago, we visited some family we hadn't seen in a while. When we got ready to leave, my son asked if he could start the truck for me. I told him that he could and continued giving hugs to my cousins. After a minute or so, my son called out for me and informed me he couldn't get the truck started without the key fab. He said, "Mommy, I need the key." I got into the truck with my purse, he pushed the button, and it started right up. That key holds the power to everything the vehicle is created to do. The vehicle cannot operate without it. It cannot perform accordingly. One of the things I like most is that if the key is removed from the truck while in motion, it signals me that there's no key, which means there isn't much longer I can go without it.

We are a vehicle in this life. We cannot operate without God. We are lifeless without God. He holds the power to everything in us that works together to do what we were purposed to do. When He is removed from our decisions, purpose, thinking, and lifestyle, there's only so far we can go without Him. Call out for Him and tell Him that you need Him so that you can get reconnected. We cannot operate as we were designed to without our power source. God is the key; don't leave home without Him!

Reflection:

What weaknesses in your life need God's power?

_____

_____

_____

_____

_____

_____

_____

_____

_____

_____

_____

_____

_____

Day Twenty Nine

Have I not commanded you?
Be strong and courageous.
Do not be afraid; do not be
discouraged, for the Lord
your God will be with you
wherever you go."

Joshua 1:9

A friend of mine recently made some work-related changes. She'd been doing the same job for a while and wanted to branch out and do something different. As with any new transition, you question if you made the right decision; you wonder if you will like or adjust well to the change. Not long after starting her new job, she told me that she had done something new and out of the ordinary. I was quite surprised and excited to learn that she led a professional development session for her colleagues. I've known her for years, but I've rarely seen her operate in that capacity. As soon as I saw her message, my initial response in my mind was, "Growth!"

There are times when we've been in a certain environment for so long that things become stagnant; we become stagnant. This can cause us to lose sight of our potential. But growth can take place when removed from that environment and positioned in a place where you are nurtured and reminded of who you are. Don't allow fear and complacency to keep you from being all that God has created you to be. There is greater in you. You have to be willing to let some things go to let your potential be revealed. Remove yourself from the people and environments that stifle your calling. Be bold and courageous as you walk out your gifts.

Reflection:

How have you operated in fear that has kept you from being bold and courageous?

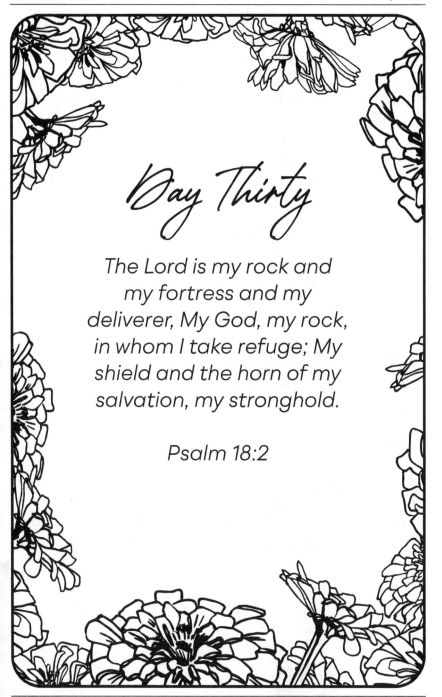

Day Thirty

The Lord is my rock and my fortress and my deliverer, My God, my rock, in whom I take refuge; My shield and the horn of my salvation, my stronghold.

Psalm 18:2

My ride home from work is usually when I decompress and reflect. It's typically pretty uneventful. But, one day, on my drive from work, I was heading to pick up my kids and noticed a power outage in the area. I approached a childcare center at one of the stop lights. In the building, they were in complete darkness. As I sat at the light, I observed parent after parent pull into the parking lot, somewhat frantic. These parents were anxious and scared for their child's safety. They did not know if their children were okay, if they were afraid of being in the dark, or if more could be going on, and the teachers didn't know because it was so dark. As a parent, I could relate to their concern. As I watched parents run to the entrance, I could see through one of the windows in the building that someone in one of the rooms had a flashlight. They were using their light to see and escort the kids out of the environment. This was a powerful moment because someone cared enough about getting these kids out of this dark environment and ensuring they were placed in a safe space.

God is just so good that he uses those moments to show us just how much he cares for us. God has done the same thing for us. He took us out of darkness and brought us to the safety of His arms. He brought us out of the traps the enemy set for us. He allowed us to see just how much better life is under the precious light and life of Jesus Christ. We don't have to wander around with uncertainty. He is our refuge.

Reflection:

What would your life be like without the light of Jesus Christ?

_____

_____

_____

_____

_____

_____

_____

_____

_____

_____

_____

_____

About The Author

Sparkle Jones is a native of Tulsa, Oklahoma. She was raised at Greater St. John A.M.E. (African Methodist Episcopal) Church. At the age of 16, she joined Friendship Church in Tulsa, OK. It was during her time there that she grew to have a stronger relationship with God and desired to grow deeper in the Word.

In 2004, Sparkle moved to Houston, TX to be closer to her family. She became an active member at The Fountain of Praise Church where she was an active part of the music ministry. Soon after moving to Houston, Sparkle met Pastor Carlos Jones II and the two quickly became friends. In 2010, Sparkle and Pastor Carlos became engaged and married. The couple now share three beautiful children, Summer, and Carlos III, and Carson.

When most people think of a pastor's wife, they envision someone sitting on the first row with a big hat. However, when you visit Inspiration Church, that is not what you will find. Sparkle Jones is the quiet force supporting her husband and ensuring everything is running well. On Sunday mornings, she can be found singing with the praise and worship team. Once she hops off the stage, her passion for children take her to work in the position she loves the most as the Children's Ministry Leader. Each week, she provides the children of the church the spiritual food they need to have a successful week.

Sparkle uses her experiences, such as the loss of a pregnancy, to reach others who have gone through similar experiences. She shares God's love where needed and has the innate ability to connect with others and build relationships. Sparkle considers it a privilege to serve the ministry alongside her husband, Pastor Carlos. She will continue to be active in ministry at Inspiration Church as long as God allows.

She is in her 13th year in education. She graduated from Northeastern State University with a Bachelor of Business Administration in Management. She also received her Master of Education in Education Administration from Lamar University. Sparkle holds educational certifications in the areas of Generalist 4-8, Special Education EC-12, and Principal Certification.

Sparkle can be reached at
Sparklejones@myyahoo.com

CPSIA information can be obtained
at www.ICGtesting.com
Printed in the USA
BVHW070001120123
655994BV00011B/575